An Introduction to Garden Feng Shui

Contents

Introduction

Feng shui is the ancient Chinese art of designing your surroundings to influence your health, success and happiness. It is a way of being in control of your own life; taking action to change the things you are not satisfied with, and capitalizing on the aspects of your life which you like. Today, many people have learnt to practise feng shui in their homes by rearranging their living space and furniture, redecorating, changing the use of certain rooms and so on. But feng shui is every bit as important in the garden as it is indoors. It is no good having a perfect house if your garden is an overgrown mess. If you want every aspect of your life to benefit from good feng shui, you must use feng shui in every part of your property.

Improve Your Life and Your Garden

Not only will good feng shui in the garden bring you benefits in your life in general, it will also have the more specific - but also important - advantage of improving your garden as a place to spend your time. The principles of good feng shui are a good set of principles for garden design, too. A good feng shui garden is also an attractive and pleasant garden for whatever purpose you want: for meditating, for entertaining friends, for your children to play safely, or simply for relaxing.

The principle behind feng shui is that positive cosmic energy, or ch'i, needs to flow smoothly and freely through its surroundings in order to create harmony. This book explains how to improve the flow of ch'i in your own garden. We will look at all the features which go to make up a garden, and consider how each can be used or adapted to maximize good feng shui. These features will include:

- the shape of the garden
- entrances and boundaries
- light and shade
- flower beds, lawns, paths and patios
- garden buildings
- water features
- seats and arbours
- statues and ornaments
- plants in the garden.

You will see from this list that although plants are, of course, important in the garden, there are all sorts of other features which matter too. It is perfectly possible to have a garden with virtually no plants in it - especially if you have only a small space - and this does not mean that it cannot have good feng shui. The flow of ch'i is certainly affected by plants, but it is just as strongly influenced by paths or buildings, open spaces or brightly coloured ornaments.

Western Gardens and Feng Shui

There is a common (and understandable) misconception that a good feng shui garden must be an Eastern garden; it must be Chinese or Japanese, perhaps even covered in raked gravel like the Japanese Zen gardens. But this isn't so at all. Zen gardens are certainly designed on feng shui principles and they are an excellent example of feng shui gardening - but an extreme one.

You can apply feng shui principles to any kind of garden, just as you can apply them to any kind of house. You don't have to live in a Chinese courtyard house with turned-up eaves in the Chinese style to use feng shui at home. And neither are you obliged to have gravel or Japanese maple trees in your garden if you don't care for them.

Many classic styles of gardening lend themselves extremely well to feng shui, from Italian Renaissance gardens or walled courtyards to parterres, vegetable gardens or classic English gardens. As you will see in this Introduction to Garden Feng Shui you can have a feng shui garden whether you own a window box or a country estate.

Chapter 1 – Principles of Feng Shui

Before you can apply feng shui to the garden, you need to know how feng shui works. Feng shui is not difficult or complicated to learn, but there is quite a lot of information to cover. It would be perfectly possible to spend this entire book looking at the basics of feng shui, without ever mentioning gardens at all.

This chapter, therefore, is as basic as it gets. It will include all the information you need to follow the rest of the book, but it is not a complete guide to feng shui. We will simply look at the key elements which you need to understand and how they interrelate.

Ch'i

Central to feng shui is the concept of ch'i. This is an Eastern concept, with no direct Western parallel, but it is not too difficult for Western minds to grasp. Ch'i is universal energy, or life force, and the Chinese believe that it flows through, in and around everything. Probably the nearest Western equivalent to ch'i is the Christian concept of the Holy Spirit. We contain ch'i within our own bodies; it is in trees and plants and animals. It is also in the air around us, flowing through our homes, work places, gardens and everywhere else.

This is the essence of feng shui. It is all about providing ch'i with the best environment to flow freely; not too slow or it will stagnate, not too fast or it will become too energetic and unrelaxed. *Feng shui* means 'wind' and 'water', and ch'i likes to move in much the same way as do wind and water. It likes to meander in gentle curves, with enough space to move freely, but it enjoys exploring occasional inlets and secret spaces which are accessible, and rippling or eddying from time to time.

Yin and Yang

Feng shui originally developed as part of Taoism (pronounced dowism), the ancient religion of China. The Tao means the Way and the Tao is the source of everything in the universe. According to the Taoists, everything there is can be divided into heaven or earth, spirit or matter, yang or yin. These two opposites form a balance in nature, and ch'i is kept in motion by a constant movement from one to the other, much in the same way as an alternating electrical current is created.

But the Taoists understand that there are no absolutes in this world and that there is always an element of yin within any yang force or object, and vice versa. This is why, when they depict yin and yang in their best-known symbol, there is always a dot of white yang within the black yin, and a dot of black yin within the white yang.

Yin	**Yang**
Structure	Function
Night	Day
Cold	Hot
Earth	Sky
Moon	Sun
Slow	Fast
Humidity	Dryness
Ascends energy	Descends energy
Fluids	Energy
Calm	Expressive
Death	Birth

The yin/yang symbol is always shown the same way up. The white yang is at the top representing summer and the south (the sunny direction), while the bottom, yin, half of the symbol represents winter and the north. You will find throughout this book that in feng shui south is at the top of the compass and north is at the bottom; this is the way the Chinese compass is designed.

In feng shui, you need to keep a balance of yin and yang in order to help the ch'i to flow. So what is yin and what is yang in your garden? Well, everything is predominantly either one or the other, but the clearest example is that light is yang and dark is yin. So you are looking for a balance of light and shade in any garden. Here are a few more examples of yang and yin:

Yang	Yin
Sun	Shade
Male	Female
Summer	Winter
Hot	Cold
Dry	Wet
Hard	Soft
Sky	Earth
Active	Passive
Bright colour	Muted colour
Exposed	Enclosed

The Five Elements

In the West, we often talk about the four elements of fire, water, air and earth, of which people used to believe everything was made up, and which are still used in astrology. In the East they have a similar approach, except that the Eastern system has five elements: fire, water, wood, metal and earth. Each of these elements is ascribed a direction in feng shui:

- Fire: south
- Water: north
- Wood: east
- Metal: west
- Earth: centre.

The relevance of these elements in feng shui will become more apparent later in this book, where you will find that there is often a reason to use an object made of a certain element in a certain part of the garden. The correct element will usually be selected on the basis of whether the place you are using it is in the north, south, east, west or centre of the garden.

The Four animals

Each of the four cardinal compass directions is accorded an animal. These animals symbolize the nature or mood of that direction. We have already seen how ch'i flows in and around everything. It stands to reason that when ch'i reaches your garden, it will bear the stamp of the place it has come from. And although it will make a difference whether it arrives at your garden via a cemetery or a peaceful park, it will also be strongly influenced simply by the direction from which it arrives.

Ch'i enters your garden constantly from all directions and the four animals of the compass give you a big clue to the type of ch'i which is reaching your garden.

- The Red Phoenix of the South

The phoenix is the most yang of the animals, since it lives in the yang, south part of the compass. The ch'i in the south part of your garden will arrive influenced by this creature, with its eternal optimism and ability to overcome even death and to rise again from the ashes. Ch'i from the south is therefore expansive, lucky, positive, happy, light and full of life, energy and hope.

- The Black Tortoise of the North

This is a slow animal and brings sleepy, yin ch'i to the north of your garden. However, it is a kindly creature and the ch'i is wintery and mysterious, but nevertheless nurturing and caring.

- The Green Dragon of the East

You need to understand the Chinese view of dragons to understand this creature. The Chinese dragon is kind, cultured and wise, and the ch'i entering the east of your garden is protective, kindly and full of wisdom. This is the creature of the spring; livelier than the tortoise but more reserved than the outgoing phoenix.

- The White Tiger of the West

This is a dangerous and unpredictable animal and one to be treated with extreme caution. As we shall see later, it is generally wise to reduce the flow of ch'i into the west of your garden and to calm it down as it enters. Otherwise you may feel the violent, stormy side of this creature of the autumn. On the other hand, a little of this ch'i from the west can sometimes be just what you need to prod things into life and ensure that your garden - and your life - don't stagnate.

The Eight Enrichments

In order to feng shui any area - a house, a garden, a single room or whatever - it is divided (notionally) into eight areas, known as the eight enrichments. Each of these relates to a different aspect of your life. These should form into eight equal divisions crossing diagonally at a single point in the centre, like slices of a cake.

The eight enrichments are generally presented on paper as a circle or octagon divided into eight segments but, of course, few gardens or houses are actually circular or octagonal. So you need to divide a plan of your garden into eight as accurately as you can, even if it is square or rectangular; simply work out where the middle is and divide it into sections which cross at this point.

Some areas which you might want to feng shui may be very irregular, perhaps L-shaped or T-shaped. These still follow the same principle, but you will find that some of the eight enrichments have no garden to match them; or they have extra garden projecting beyond them. We'll be looking at how to feng shui this kind of space in Chapter 3.

Each of the eight enrichments is concerned with a different aspect of your life. In order to harmonize that aspect, you need to harmonize the feng shui in that area of your house and your garden. The eight enrichments are:

- Fame
- Health and peace
- Pleasure and indulgence
- Friends and new beginnings
- Relationship
- Children and family

- Wisdom and experience
- Wealth.

Suppose you are having financial problems. You would need to look at the feng shui of your wealth enrichment and see how you can improve it. This, in turn, will improve your fortunes in money matters.

Each of the eight enrichments has a particular compass direction in which it is at home. Fame, for example, has its natural home in the south, where it can expand and be outgoing. Children and family are sited in the north-east, between the wise Green Dragon and the nurturing Black Tortoise; where better to deal with matters concerning your children? The diagram on the previous page shows where each of the eight enrichments belongs.

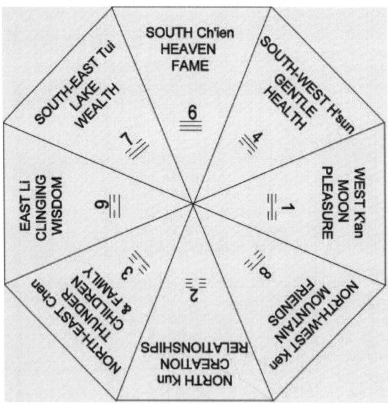

The eight enrichments

The Pah Kwa

In order to work out the feng shui for your garden, house or wherever, you need to lay a diagram of the eight enrichments, over a plan of the area in question. This diagram is known as the Pah Kwa. This enables you to see which part of the garden each enrichment aligns with; in other words which part of the garden influences each aspect of your life. So the question is: how do you align the Pah Kwa?

The answer is: it depends which way the garden faces. You position the Pah Kwa so that the main entrance to the garden (or whatever area you are dealing with) has the fame enrichment sitting over it. If the entrance to your garden happens to be in the south, this means that the fame enrichment will be in its natural home - and so will all the others.

If the entrance faces any other way, however, the fame enrichment will not face south - and the other enrichments will also be out of line with their natural homes. But this is fine – it happens in the majority of gardens. According to the Chinese, you should ideally have a home and a garden which face south, but if you don't, any disadvantages can easily be remedied; that's what feng shui is all about.

Many gardens have only one entrance, often from the house through the back door, and it is obvious that this is the part of the plan which must line up with the fame enrichment. But some gardens have more than one contender for the position of 'main' entrance. If there is more than one way in and out of your garden, which should you treat as the main one?

The solution is really to stop thinking about it too hard and start to feel it. Use your intuition. Which entrance feels like the main one?

This is your garden and its feng shui will affect your life, so what matters is the way it feels to you. It says something about you, which is important for feng shui, if you regard the side entrance to your garden as being more significant than the front entrance, for example. Or the French doors from the living room as being more important than the back door from the kitchen. The main entrance is the one which you feel is the main one.

You are actually laying the Pah Kwa so that the fame enrichment aligns with the direction in which the garden faces. Almost always this means the main entrance, but just occasionally a garden very obviously faces a different way. Perhaps the main entrance is from the house, but the garden is on a cliff looking out to sea, or on the slope of a hill with a beautiful vista looking away from the house. In either of these cases, you will probably feel instinctively that the garden faces the sea, or the panoramic view, rather than the entrance from the house. If this is so, go with your feelings. Line up the fame enrichment over the part of the garden which faces the sea or the view.

TASK

Intuition is very important to feng shui. The way you feel about a space is intricately bound up with the mood that space inspires in you and the effect it has on your life. As well as deciding which way your own garden faces - whether or not you feel it faces the main entrance to it - visit other gardens, including those open to the public and spend some time thinking about which way they face.

If you visit a garden within a park, or one open to the public which may have several gardens within it, it is often quite unclear at first glance which way it faces. These kinds of gardens often have more than one entrance, for a start.

Stand in the garden and allow yourself to sense, rather than analyse, the feel of the garden. Ask yourself:

- Which way does this garden seem to face?

- If this were my garden, which way would I design it to face?

When you visit friends, try to get a feel of which way their garden faces, especially if it isn't obvious. Try asking them which way they feel it faces, and why. There is no right or wrong - you feel what you feel - and it doesn't matter whether they feel the same way as you or not. The important thing is to learn to sense the feel of a space intuitively rather than rely on analysing it according to lessons from books – this one or any other. The books are an important guide, but it is your feelings

Chapter 2 – Feng Shui Remedies in the Garden

One of the great things about feng shui is that almost no problem area, however bad its feng shut, is irredeemable. You can identify areas where the ch'i is slowing and stagnating, or areas where it is too energized, but you can always do something about them.

If the ch'i is moving too slowly, the area of your life governed by the enrichment the slow ch't is in will also stagnate. If, for example, there is an area of stagnant ch'i in your relationship enrichment, it is likely that you will not be in a relationship, or you will be in one which seems to be going nowhere.

If, on the other hand, the ch'i is moving too fast, or is forced into a straight, funnelled path, your life will be overactive and unpredictable in this area. To take the case of the relationship enrichment again, ch'i moving too fast may give you a tempestuous and insecure relationship.

Identifying Bad Feng Shui

How are you supposed to know if the ch'i isn't flowing freely? Well, there are two ways. The first is to think about the area of your life governed by each enrichment in turn. If you are quite happy with it - your relationship, wealth, children or whichever - don't tamper with the feng shui of that enrichment too much; it is clearly fine. If you are not happy with a particular part of your life, the feng shui of that enrichment clearly isn't right.

The other way to assess the feng shui of any particular area is to look at the space in question. If you have used the first approach to establish that there is a problem in a particular enrichment, you will still need to use this approach to identify what exactly the problem is.

Throughout this book we'll be looking at particular features and layouts that you should either cultivate or avoid in your garden, but in general the best approach is to stand in the enrichment, or wander around it, and imagine you are the ch'i. Are there areas which seem dark or impenetrable? If so, the ch'i will encounter the same problem and will slow down or stagnate altogether. Are there places where you feel too exposed or lost in the middle of a large expanse of open space? Or where you feel you are being funnelled down a particular route? If so, the ch'i will encounter the same problem, and is likely to become too fast or over-stimulated.

The Eight Remedies

Having identified problem areas, you will need to introduce remedies. Where the ch'i is too slow or sleepy, you will need to perk it up a bit. Where it is accelerating too fast, you will need to calm it down. There are eight types of remedy used in feng shui, and you can choose a suitable one for your purpose:

- Light
- Straight line
- Stillness
- Sound
- Movement
- Colour
- Functional device
- Life

Each remedy has a particular compass direction to which it belongs, but you can use any remedy in any part of the garden for which it is suitable. Where possible, though, try to use a remedy in the part of the garden where it is at home. Remember, too, that each compass direction has its own element. If you can select a remedy which is made of, or incorporates, the appropriate element for that part of your garden, better still. But again, any remedy is better than none. Just make sure you pick a calming remedy where the ch'i is overstimulated and an enlivening remedy where it is too slow.

Light

Ch'i likes a balance of light and shade - yin and yang - but it resists venturing into dark areas, so you are likely to encounter problems if you have any very overgrown or shaded areas in your garden. The way to encourage the ch'i into these spaces and get it flowing freely again is to use a light remedy.

The most simple remedy in a lot of these situations is to cut back or clear the area, remove the undergrowth and let the light and air into the space. But there are also other solutions, especially where the darkness is not caused by undergrowth or overhanging branches, but by high walls or garden buildings. You could introduce plants with silver-coloured foliage such as artemisias or a eucalyptus tree. You could paint a nearby wall or side of a shed white or some other pale colour to reflect more light into the area. Or you could add a mirror, or a water feature which will reflect light.

The other obvious solution is to use lights themselves. You can either add electric lights in your garden, or go for a more natural solution with lanterns and candles. This approach works particularly well if the area is light enough for the ch'i to flow smoothly at midday, but becomes sombre when it is out of the sun by late afternoon.

Light remedies are especially at home in the south part of the garden, which is also the area where the element of fire belongs. So a light remedy which incorporates fire - such as a candle lantern – is particularly appropriate for waking up the ch'i in the south part of the garden.

Straight line

This is another remedy for sleepy or stagnating ch'i. You can wake this kind of ch'i up by creating a straight line to direct it along. The straight line can be either horizontal or vertical - you can usually tell instinctively which direction you most want to direct the ch'i.

Straight-line remedies in the garden can be created using straight plants such as bamboo or foxgloves, which have a spiky outline that helps to prod the ch'i into life. You can also use a straight, vertical water jet from a fountain to create the same effect, or a straight water channel like a small canal. Paths can be laid straight in an area of stagnating ch'i, and low walls, hedges or the edges of flower beds can also follow a direct straight line instead of curving.

There is a wide range of garden ornaments and features which incorporate straight lines and can be used as remedies, such as trellis, children's slides, hammocks, washing lines, obelisks, beanpoles, and garden furniture made from slatted wood. Straight-line remedies are most at home in the south-west part of the garden.

Stillness

Where ch'i is overactive, you can calm it down by creating an area of stillness. A large, solid urn, pot or statue, or perhaps an aged and weathered boulder or rock, will create a stillness remedy. A calm, still, round pond will have the same effect.

This remedy is most at home in the west, where it helps to calm the unpredictable energy of the White Tiger. If you are using a stillness remedy in the west, you could combine it with metal, since this is the element of the west. For example, a large iron ball, or a metal urn.

Sound

Noise is a good way of introducing energy into ch'i which has become too slow. In dark or overcrowded parts of the garden, bring in a sound remedy. You could use plants which make a noise, such as quivering aspen trees or bamboo. Or hang wind -Chimes or bring in the sound of water in a waterfall or fountain.

Another way to introduce sound is to encourage wildlife such as birds, by putting a bird table in the area. Or plant lavender and listen to the sound of the bees. If you have children, you could put their slide, swings or sandpit here, and you are likely to find that the noise level goes up considerably. Sound remedies are at their best in the north-west of the garden.

Movement

If the ch'i is too slow moving, another way to encourage it is with a movement remedy. These include plants which move in the slightest breeze, such as ornamental grasses, or wind chimes, mobiles or other objects which will sway or swing in the breeze. You might want to try using flags, or even smoke from the bonfire or barbecue.

You can also use any water feature in which the water is moving, such as a stream or a water spout. Water features are particularly useful as movement remedies in the north, since both the remedy and the element of water are at home here.

Colour

Colour can be used either to slow down or to speed up ch'i, depending on whether you use a bright, invigorating colour or a peaceful pastel. Bear in mind that a dazzling white, often thought of as a calm colour, can actually be bright and energizing, especially if it catches the sun. If you want to calm the ch'i down, it is better to go for an off-white or cream rather than a pure white.

You can obviously introduce a colour remedy through plants, bearing in mind that foliage and berries - and sometimes even bark – are often as strongly coloured as flowers. But there are lots of other ways you can bring colour to an area. For a start, you can paint or stain furniture, fences, walls, trellis and pots. You can even paint a mural on the garden wall.

You can use coloured, glazed pots or tiles, or even mosaics set into a patio or path. A water feature such as a birdbath or fishpond could have coloured ceramic or tiles, and paths can be made from coloured bricks, gravel, stones or sand. Encouraging birds into an area will bring colour to it, as will putting goldfish in a pond.
There is almost no end to the ornaments you can have in your garden, which can be coloured: shells, crystals, fairy lights, stained glass, ribbon and flags. And don't forget regular features of many gardens such as the car in the driveway, the children's toys, or washing hanging on a line.

Colour remedies can be used anywhere they are needed, but they are most effective in the north-east part of the garden.

Functional **Device**

Ch'i which is inclined to become sluggish will be enlivened by introducing a functional object. All sorts of regular garden items are functional, such as a lawnmower, a sundial, a barbecue, a garden light, a windmill birdscarer or a dustbin. If you want water in this part of the garden you could have a well, a fountain, a birdbath or even a garden tap.

Functional devices work best in the east, which is also the direction of wood, so you could combine the two with, say, a wooden compost heap.

Life

Anything alive and moving will help to keep ch'i moving in an otherwise sleepy part of the garden. Plants are obvious life remedies to use in a garden, but there are others. Try installing a fish pond, encouraging birds with a feeder or a birdbath, or bringing in insects by planting scented plants such as lavender. Children are lively too, so you could put some of their toys here and let them liven the area up for you. Life remedies are at their best in the south-east.

TASK

Have a look round your garden and draw up a list of all the movable objects in it. These might be anything from benches and pots to lawnmowers and wind chimes. Add to the list anything you want for your garden but haven't yet acquired, which you could choose to site wherever you like - things such as a built-in barbecue, a rose arch or a water feature.

Now go through this list and mark by each item what kind of remedy or remedies it could be. For example, a garden light could be used as a light remedy or as a functional device. Depending on its design; it might even be a straight-line remedy as well.

When you come to feng shut your garden, you will need this list. Whenever you find area which needs a remedy, you can go through this list to find the most useful item to place in the area to function as the remedy you need.

Chapter 3 – The Shape of the Garden

The overall shape of your garden is important because when you overlay the Pah Kwa on it, it will tell you whether any enrichments are missing or enlarged. This, in turn, will be reflected in your life. A missing children and family section, for example, often indicates that you have no children, or that you are estranged from them. An overlarge children and family enrichment, on the other hand, is often present in the gardens of people with very large families.

How Many Gardens Do You Have?

You might have a front garden and a back garden. Or a bit of garden round the side of the house. Or maybe a section of garden which leads off the main garden. Should you work out the feng shui for each garden independently of the rest, or should you treat them all as one oddly shaped garden?

If the gardens really are completely separate, treat them as separate gardens for feng shui purposes. If you have garden all around your house, treat the whole plot - house and garden - as one and feng shui the whole lot together (this arrangement is considered perfect by the Chinese). But what about all those other quirky gardens which don't quite fit either of these descriptions? The answer to this lies with your own feelings. This is your garden; do you think of it as one complete garden, or as two (or more) separate gardens? This is the determining factor in deciding how to feng shui this kind of garden.

People who like to keep separate parts of their life well apart – not socializing with work colleagues, for example - tend to view separate areas of garden as being independent. People who have a more integrated approach to life will often view their whole garden as one unit even when others might see it as two or more gardens. So the way you choose to feng shui this kind of garden says as much about you as it does about the space.

How Does The House Fit In?

Many people are confused about how the feng shui of their garden interrelates with the feng shui of their house. If you have created perfect feng shui in your house, on what are you missing out in your life by not ensuring good feng shui in your garden? For a start, the ch'i which reaches your house arrives via your garden, so you want to give it the most harmonious influence you can en route. But there's more to it than that.

There is a subtle difference between the feng shui of your house and that of your garden in terms of their influence on your life. Your house, which is a kind of inner sanctum, is concerned with your personal, private attitudes and feelings. The more public garden, on the other hand, represents the things which are outside you and around you; the people and influences which affect you.

For example, take the wealth enrichment of your house and garden. This area of your house governs your personal approach to money; whether you spend or save, whether you summon up the nerve to ask for a raise, how generous you are, and so on. The wealth enrichment in your garden is more concerned with influencing outside people and forces: will your investments prosper, will your boss decide you deserve a raise, will a lucrative new job offer materialize?

If you are treating the house and garden as one unit for feng shui purposes, you will need to lay the Pah Kwa over the whole plot. Some enrichments will fall in the house, others in the garden – and some in both. Again, the house indicates a more private aspect of the enrichment than the garden; enrichments which fall entirely in the house show that you treat that aspect of your life privately. Conversely, an enrichment which falls in the garden indicates that only the aspect of your life in question is public.

Suppose your wisdom and experience enrichment is entirely in the house. You probably keep a lot of your past very quiet, or perhaps you have a private approach to increasing your knowledge and education. Maybe you like to learn a lot by reading privately, or perhaps you take correspondence courses. If, on the other hand, the wisdom and experience enrichment all falls within the garden, you are probably very public about it. Perhaps you give talks about your experiences, or you use your knowledge as a teacher or trainer.

Irregular Shaped Gardens

If your garden is not a square or a circle, or something fairly close, you may well find that the Pah Kwa does not fit over it exactly. Either some parts of the Pah Kwa have no garden at all ascribed to them, or they have so much that part of it projects beyond the edge of your Pah Kwa. Many gardens fit into this category, of course. So what does it mean?

If you think about it, it is quite obvious what it means. The eight enrichments of the Pah Kwa simply represent parts of your life, so an empty or overfull section means that the aspect of your life in question is either empty or too full. Suppose your friends and new beginnings enrichment has no garden correlating with it. This suggests that you have few friends. This may not be as depressing as it sounds; some people would rather have only a few close friends, and cannot be bothered with social acquaintances. If this is you, leave your garden alone. If, however, you would like more of a social life, you can remedy the missing section, as we will see in a moment. This enrichment also represents new beginnings; if it is missing, you may find that you tend to stick with things as they are, rather than start new projects. Again, you may be quite happy with this, or you may not.

If your friends and new beginnings enrichment is particularly large, protruding beyond the Pah Kwa, you most probably have a busy social life and frequently start new projects. Again, you may enjoy this lifestyle, or you may find it too exhausting and demanding, and wish you could ease up a bit.

So what do you do if you are not happy with an enrichment being absent or being too large? You can create the effect of an absent (or very small) section by placing a mirror against the boundary where the missing section would have been. When you look at the mirror, it will give the impression that you are looking into the missing enrichment.

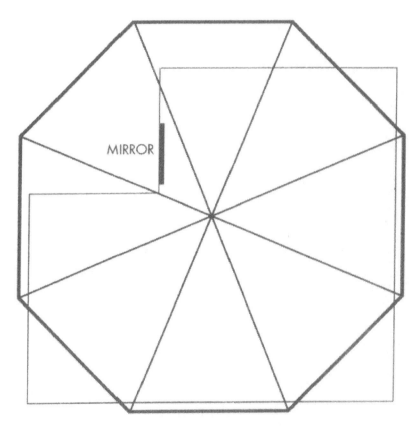

Position a mirror to create a missing section or enlarge one that is too small

If a part of the garden is over-large and the enrichment is creating an overcrowded part of your life, you need to do something about this, too. It should not be necessary to go to such extremes as getting rid of the extra section of garden. If you want to clear some space in your life, symbolize this by clearing space in the relevant section of the garden. If your relationship enrichment is oversized, and your relationship is taking up too much of your attention by being traumatic or stormy or obsessive, clear up the relevant section of your garden. Tidy it and keep it free of clutter, and don't have too many features or ornaments in there. Don't make it boring, but keep it simple and easy to maintain; your relationship should follow suit.

Using the Eight Enrichments

The next stage in applying feng shui to your garden is to look at what you use each section of the garden for. You need to suit each activity to the best enrichment you can. For instance, do you have a barbecue? Which enrichment is it in? If it is in your wealth enrichment, you are burning money every time you light it. It would be much better to put it in the pleasure and indulgence section, or in the friends and new beginnings enrichment if you usually light it when you are entertaining. It is also suited to the south or southeast of the garden, since these are the directions of the fire element.

What about the children's swings or sandpit? Try to put these in the children and family enrichment. Grow herbs in the health and happiness enrichment, and so on. Here is an idea of the kind of activities and features which suit each enrichment of the garden:

Fame
This is the area for building your reputation, so use it to entertain people you are trying to impress. Put your house name in the fame enrichment of your front garden. You could also use this part of the garden for growing giant vegetables or prize plants which you want to show off. Don't try to do anything private here as you are likely to be disturbed; it is not the place for a quiet seat for meditating or reading.

Health and happiness

Have your quiet seat for resting and relaxing here, perhaps to the sound of water. This is also the place to grow herbs for healing and for fresh, healthy cooking. You might want a vegetable garden here, too.

Pleasure and indulgence

Have your best fun in this part of the garden. This is a good spot for the barbecue, and for a table and chairs. Or you could put a swimming pool here. If you can't afford a swimming pool, a simple hammock would suit this enrichment. If you enjoy more private pursuits, this is the spot for your dream garden if you are a gardener - the one you really want to spend lots of time tending.

Friends and new beginnings

This is another good area for the barbecue, or for seating. Or if you and your friends are more active, put up the badminton net here. It is also a good spot for a greenhouse or a seed bed, where you start off new plants. You could keep your dustbins here to symbolize a continual throwing out of the old to make way for the new.

Relationship

What do you and your partner enjoy doing together in the garden? Whatever it is, this is the place to do it. So put a romantic seat here under a bower, or the greenhouse if you like to work in the greenhouse together. This is the place for activities you share with your partner. If you are single and would like a relationship, keep this area tidy and free of weeds. Plant perennial rather than annual flowers, and a fruit tree which will blossom and bear fruit.

Children and family

If you have children, grandchildren, or frequent visitors with children, this is the place to make safe for them. Don't grow any poisonous or thorny plants here, and make sure fences and boundaries are safe and secure. This is the area for a sandpit, a swing, a tree house or a paddling pool, or simply a lawn where the kids can play with a ball.

Wisdom and experience

Use this part of the garden to learn and grow. Grow new plants here in trial beds, or have a private seat where you sit and read or meditate. This is also the best place to put the compost heap, where it can mature and grow into a rich mulch for your other plants.

Wealth
This means material possessions as well as money, so use this area to store things which are not just junk. You could keep your garden shed here and store garden furniture in the winter. You do not often get a choice about where to site a garage, but this is a good place for it. If you make money from your garden, for example by selling vegetables or chutneys and jams, this is the place to grow the produce if you can. Or if you keep chickens for their eggs, you could put them here.

Obviously you won't be able to do all of these things in every garden. Some enrichments may be missing, and you may have to find a second or third choice of enrichment for some activities. And it is all very well saying grow produce for selling in the wealth enrichment, and if you can you should, but if you make tomato chutney and your wealth enrichment faces north, it is not going to be a great place to grow tomatoes. So follow these guidelines as closely as you can, but don't be devastated if it doesn't work out perfectly; a second choice of enrichment, and often a third, will usually be fine.

Garden Boundaries

You have no control over the ch'i arriving in your garden until it reaches your boundary. So the way to plan your boundaries, and choose between walls, trellis, fences, hedges and so on, is to assess the ch'i arriving in your garden along each side, and to suit the boundary to this.

The first thing to consider is the direction from which the ch'i is coming. In the absence of any other significant influences, you should gauge the boundary to this.

South boundary
You generally want to let in the open, expansive south ch'i of the Red Phoenix, but it can be too much if you have no boundary at all. So have an

open boundary along the south edge of your garden. Avoid dense hedges and high fences and walls, and opt instead for trellis, an open hedge, railings, or a low wall with a line of trees along it.

North boundary
Ch'i from the north is sleepy and the Black Tortoise needs encouragement to bring you the nurturing north ch'i. Again, you need to encourage it by keeping this boundary as open and free as possible. In particular, clear any dense or overhanging branches which will encourage it to stagnate.

East boundary
Another direction from which to encourage ch'i, but the one danger with the wise Green Dragon is that its influence will be so fertile that your garden will be overrun from the east and become too overgrown. So keep the ch'i in check with an open boundary and don't use very low walls - go for waist height rather than knee height.

West boundary
The White Tiger needs keeping strongly in check, of course, or you could easily let in too much dangerous, unpredictable ch'i. This is the boundary for using a full-height solid fence, wall or dense hedge (which must stay dense through the winter if it is to remain effective). By the way, don't provoke the White Tiger with a spiky hedge such as holly or berberis; use something softer such as privet or yew. If you try to block out the ch'i from the west entirely you may provoke it, so it is a good idea to give it the occasional opportunity to enter, allowing it a safety valve to prevent it building up too much. You could use a fence with the odd knot hole, or if you have a gate on this wall, find one with a design which is not completely solid, but has a few gaps for the ch'i to enter through.

These guidelines are a kind of default setting if there are no other important influences on the ch'i reaching your garden boundary. But if the ch'i is particularly good or bad, fast or slow, you will need to adapt your boundaries to take account of this.

Good ch'i
If any of your boundaries face a particularly beautiful area with good feng shui - such as a park or a lovely country view - you can open up the boundary more than you would do otherwise to let in the influences of the good neighbouring feng shui.

Bad ch'I (known as sha)
If ch'i reaching your garden has recently passed through an army firing range, an abbatoir, a dirty, noisy factory or some other negative influence, respond by creating a more solid or higher boundary to block some or all of its influence.

Fast ch'I
If the ch'i arrives flowing downhill towards you, or along a straight road pointing at your garden, it will be too accelerated. Slow it down with a boundary which breaks its flow, such as a hedge, or a trellis which is well covered with climbing plants (in winter as well as summer).

Slow ch'I
Ch'i which arrives by winding through narrow alleys, or which has to negotiate a tall building opposite your boundary, will have been slowed down. If it is basically beneficial ch'i, you need to encourage it into the garden by removing any inhibiting boundary or overgrown branches, and opening up this side of your garden as much as possible.

The Garden Entrance

The main entrance - and any others - should be welcoming to ch'i and visitors alike. And, of course, to you. Create an entrance which invites you to spend time in your garden. The shape of the main entrance pathway from the boundary to the house is important. You don't want to funnel ch'i through the entrance and then down a straight path to the door. Much better to have a curving path to encourage the ch'i, whether you have a driveway or a simple footpath.
As with boundaries, consider what influence you want to have over the ch'i as it enters your garden, and have a gate of a suitable height and design. Solid doors block ch'i completely and should be avoided in the west. Otherwise, when you open the gate the ch'i will rush in angrily.
You can choose wooden or metal gates, painted brightly to stimulate ch'i, or in soft colours to calm it, or left natural. A curving design in the wood

or metalwork is good for ch'i, but if you want to pep up the ch'i, use a design which incorporates straight lines.

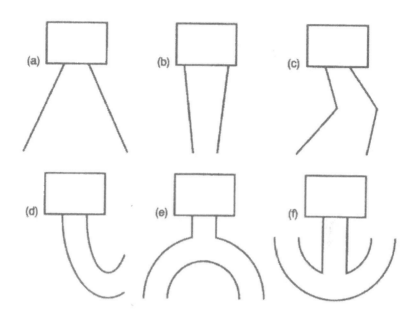

Different types of drive: a, band c are difficult feng shui while d, e and f are beneficial

In general, gates should not be left open. If the gate is needed, it should be used. The only possible exception to this is the south entrance. If a narrow or dark entrance needs opening up, an open gate is more inviting than no gate at all, and symbolizes the fact that the visitor is crossing the boundary into your space. Conversely, an open south garden can acquire so much yang energy that you cannot relax. When this happens, opening a gate on to land which slopes away can let out some of the excess energy and restore the garden's balance. If you do this, you may feel you need to close the gate in the winter when the southern ch'i loses some of its exuberance.

Different compass directions obviously call for different entrances, since they each bring different kinds of ch'i. Here is idea of the kind of entrances you might want in the four main compass directions:

South entrance

This will let in lots of expansive, yang ch'i. It is great stuff, but you can have too much of it, because it is not very relaxing. Imagine looking out of the window and seeing Tiger bounding up the road to your house. You would not want to shut him out, but you might want to slow him down a bit. So this gateway should be welcoming, but not wide open. Use a full-height gate with an open design, or a half-height gate with an archway over it, or a tree planted on either side.

North entrance

This ch'i is slow and sleepy, and needs all the encouragement it can get. This is the one direction where you might not even have to have a gate at all, depending on what is beyond the garden. Certainly you should have this entrance as open as possible and clear away any overhanging branches or plants to encourage the ch'i. This entrance really should not be in the corner of the garden. If it is, could you move it a few feet along the boundary towards the middle?

West entrance

Don't encourage this ch'i, but don't provoke it by blocking it out completely. Use a full-height gate or door, preferably metal (or partly metal) since that is the element of the west, which is not completely solid but not too open in design. You should also interrupt the ch'i within a few feet of the door with some object which slows it down such as a latticework screen, or a tree or shrub ch'i has to go round.

East entrance

You want to encourage this ch'i with an open, welcoming entrance, preferably made of wood which is at home in the east. However, the one risk with this kind of ch'i is that it will be so fertile that the garden becomes completely overgrown from this side. So keep a check on it by making sure there is a gate which is kept shut.

TASK

Spend time-when you are out and about looking at the boundaries and entrances to other people's gardens as you pass them. As you drive in the car or walk down the street, think about these boundaries and entrances:

- Do they encourage you to enter?

- If so, what makes them welcoming?

- If not, what is discouraging?

Ch'i will respond in the same way that we do, so what appeals to you will also be appealing to ch'i. Make a particular note of any unusual fences, walls, hedges or entrances, whether their impact is positive or negative. You may be able to pick up ideas from other people's gateways and boundaries. If you are on a tight budget for improving the feng shui of your garden, look especially for inexpensive ideas which other people have used.

CHAPTER 4 – The Garden Layout

The first thing you need to consider when assessing the feng shui of an existing garden, or designing a new garden with good feng shui in mind, is the overall layout of the garden. Never mind the furniture or the planting or the shed or the ornaments or the pond - start with the basics.

Which bits of the garden are given over to lawn, flower beds, paths and patios? This is the place to start, and this chapter is about getting the ground plan of your garden sorted out. Once this is right, the ch'i will be flowing harmoniously around the garden as a whole, and you will have an excellent basis from which to add any features you need.

Creating a Balanced Garden

In Chapter 1 we looked at the importance of balance in the garden. You don't just want a bland, open space with no interest or texture. But neither do you want a space which is overly dark and shady, or so full of hidden corners there is nowhere in it with a visibility beyond a few feet. You need to create a balance between yin and yang; open, bright space is yang, and shady areas and secret spaces are yin.

The most important factors to balance are light and shade, and open and secret areas. You don't have to measure the exact area of shade and of sun and match them precisely; it will vary anyway according to the time of day, the time of year and the weather. Just use your instincts to judge whether you need to open up more space over here, or create a bit more shade over there.

Remember, too, that there are degrees of shade and-of openness or secrecy. A garden which alternated between bright sunlight and dense shade would feel very strange indeed. So would a wide, open lawn with small garden 'rooms' off it, each so hidden you would never find them if you did not know they were there. So encourage the ch'i from one to the other with sunlight drawing you through dappled shade and into the more solid, cool, shaded areas. Create a wide path leading from an open area which gradually narrows as it rounds a bend, leading you on to discover the secret garden beyond.

You can create sunny areas simply by clearing branches, shrubs or garden buildings, and you can add shade with trees or with pergolas or trellis screens. A pergola over a path with climbers such as roses over it can create a beautiful and inviting area of dappled shade. A secret corner can be created in the smallest of gardens, simply by making sure that the whole garden cannot be viewed at once. A simple screen or a shrub can be enough to lure the eye - and the ch'i - to investigate what is around the other side. An archway flanked by shrubs with a half-glimpsed arbour beyond is always an inviting feature and can be accommodated in all but the tiniest gardens.

Paths

Paths are an important feature of a garden, because they encourage you to explore it. And remember, what attracts you will attract the ch'i, too. As a general rule, paths should curve and meander, encouraging continuous but gentle progress through the garden.

If you have a straight path which is encouraging the ch'i to rush too fast - or you to pass through without really pausing to enjoy the garden - you can soften it by planting low-growing plants which will creep over the edge in low mounds. Saxifrages, lady's mantle, pinks and many other common garden flowers are useful for this purpose. If the path runs through a lawn, you might allow the grass to grow between the cracks in brick or paved paths, especially at the edges, to blur them.

Don't forget that you can use both vertical features and those at ground level to soften straight paths. A rose arch over a path, or a pergola, will help to interrupt the flow of ch'i and create a punctuation point in a path which is too straight. Perhaps you could even put in a gate - an open, waist-high design might well be sufficient to break up the ch'i - where the path moves from one part of the garden to another.

If a path is overly straight, it is especially important not to emphasize this further with lengthwise lines in the paving or brickwork of the path. Use a material such as gravel instead, or lay bricks in a curving pattern across rather than down the path.

You can choose the materials for your path to create a contrast with the area it runs through. Light up a shady part of the garden with a light-coloured gravel path or sandstone flags, and create a balance in a bright area by laying a darker path of slate paving or dark bricks, for example.

Sometimes, a straight path is useful. Where you want to remedy an area where the ch'i is too slow and sleepy, you can run a straight path through it to get the ch'i moving. However, you must remember that paths run in both directions. For example, a straight path leading from the east of the garden will bring a strong flow of wise, fertile ch'i to the centre of the plot. But there is also a danger that the dangerous ch'i from the west will rush down it in the other direction. So put an obstacle, or a bend in the path, at the west end of it to avoid inviting trouble from that direction.

Flower Beds

As with paths, aim to create gentle curves along the edges of flower beds and borders. If you already have a straight edge, you can either move it or simply soften it by growing plants which will spread beyond the edge of the flower bed. As with paths, straight edges to beds will speed up the ch'i in that part of the garden; use them only if this is the effect you want to achieve.

Narrow flower beds can appear mean and they don't give the ch'l room to move freely. But too wide a bed can give the ch'i no sense of flow or direction. So aim for beds which are 1 to 2 metres (3 to 7 feet) wide. Of course, if you have a huge garden with a very long flower bed you can afford to make it wider in proportion to the overall space.

Don't forget the back of the border. If it is backed by a wall or fence, make sure you soften this and add texture to it by planting shrubs or trees in front of it, or by growing climbers up it.

Island beds - completely surrounded by lawns or paths - should be curved rather than irregular in shape, and certainly should be a simple design. Round or oval beds are best, or octagonal since ch'l also likes this shape. Give Island beds a bit of height to block or partly mask the view beyond; this creates intrigue as to what is happening on the other side of the bed.

If you are trying to avoid straight lines, vegetable beds create an obvious dilemma, since these are traditionally laid out in long straight rows. The solution is to vary the direction of the lines of vegetables within the bed, and keep them fairly short. You can set out vegetables in a herringbone pattern, for instance, or offset the straight lines by planting them in a circular bed with a large round pot or urn in the middle.

Lawns and Open Spaces

Open spaces in gardens tend to be put down to lawn, but you could have a large paved or gravelled area. There is little difference in terms of how you treat them for feng shui purposes, except that grass is alive, whereas paving or gravel can seem dead. So you often need to bring life to a large area of stone with planted pots, or by encouraging seedlings in amongst the cracks in the stones. Don't ever have a large open area of concrete.

Apart from that, you need to make sure that any open area of garden is offset by smaller areas of greater interest and texture. You need to judge the size of your open space according to the amount of garden visible. A 10 metre square (33 feet square) space, if that is the entire garden, would be too much; it needs more variety to encourage the ch'i. However, if you have a garden of 2 acres, the same size lawn would be dwarfed if it were the only open area. You would need either a much larger area, or several open spaces around your 0.8 hectare (2 acre) plot.

Any open area should have curved or rounded edges rather than straight ones, and don't stop this area dead all the way round by bordering it with walls or flower beds. Allow the lawn or paving to merge, in places, into wide paths leading off it, encouraging the ch'I to explore. Don't expect the ch'i to flow out of a large space into a tiny, narrow path; you can always reduce the width of the path gradually as it progresses, creating a perspective effect which will make the path seem longer.

Any large area of lawn is best broken up a little, even if you simply break the colour of it by encouraging daisies, buttercups and violets to grow. The passion for creating a 'perfect' lawn of low-cut green without moss or flowers contradicts the principles of feng shui: all kinds of life should be encouraged, and a lawn should look like a living thing and not like a sitting-room carpet.

Another effective option for breaking up a large expanse of grass or stone is to put something in the centre of it. A gazebo or a beautiful tree with a circular seat around it, both makes an excellent focus for ch'i to flow to the centre of the space and out again. Of course, this won't go down too well with the kids if the open space is their ball games area, but you might get away with putting a swing ball or a basketball net there, which they can move out of the way temporarily when they are not using it.

Patios

Paved areas between the house and the rest of the garden can create a dead space, and one which cuts the garden off from the house. Both of these factors deter the ch'i from flowing around the patio, and can leave the house beleaguered with the ch'i inhibited from reaching it across the patio. The worst offenders are concrete patios which meet the lawn in a straight line, especially if the patio is a step above the lawn. The larger the patio area, the worse the problem.

But a patio can have good feng shui, so long as you design it the right way. For a start, use as soft a material as possible; gravel or soft-coloured brick are ideal, or wooden decking, but you can use flagstones. Next, make sure there is plenty of life. Grow creeping plants or herbs between the cracks, or take up the occasional flagstone and plant something in the gap. You can create a wonderful herb garden this way, in easy reach of the house for culinary herbs, with rosemary, sage, mint, thyme, marjoram and so on planted in amongst the stones. Or you could put plenty of pots on and around the patio and grow climbers (planted in pots) up the walls of the house.

You can also break up a large expanse of patio, and bring life to it by covering it - or just a corner or end of it - with a pergola and growing climbers over it. This also helps to bring an element of shade to the patio, balancing the bright sunshine the rest of it probably attracts.

The other important factor with patios is to make sure that they merge into the garden rather than create a psychological barrier which deters you from stepping off the edge. The edge of the patio should encourage you to step out into the garden. There are lots of ways to achieve this. Simply finishing the patio with a curved edge, such as a half circle, is more inviting than a straight edge. But you can be more inventive than this. How about wide curving steps down on to the lawn, flanked by plants in pots, to persuade you to take that step into the garden? If the patio is flagged or made of brick, and level with the grass, blur the edge of it by breaking it up so that the bricks or flags become stepping stones in the grass.

It is not difficult to create a patio which encourages ch'i around the garden and into the house, so long as you have plenty of plant life and don't create a barrier to stepping out into the rest of the garden.

TASK

Draw a rough plan of your garden or, if you are lucky enough to be designing it from scratch, draw a plan of your design so far. Include on the plan paths, flower beds, open spaces and patios, and also include any large trees or structures it would be really impossible to move.

Now start troubleshooting. Make a note of any part of the garden

where:

- the shade is dense

- there is an over-large area of open space

- there is any large area of concrete

- the ch'i is slowed down by narrow flower beds or paths, paths which are too twisting and tortuous, or excessive shade

- the ch'i is accelerated by paths which are too straight, or too wide and open, or by areas of excessive sunlight unbroken by shade.

Now go through this list and, using the suggestions in this chapter, find ways to remedy each of these problems by increasing or reducing the shade, changing paths, encouraging low-growing plants to blur the edges of paths, adding features or bringing an area to life by adding plants to it. Don't forget to use vertical features as well as horizontal ones.

Work through the list until you have found a remedy for each problem area which not only works for the feng shui of the garden, but which also helps to create a garden in which you are happy to spend time. There is no point adding features which are not to your taste. It is your garden after all, and there is more than one solution to every problem. Just keep thinking and looking for ideas until you find one which you like - you are limited only by your imagination.

CHAPTER 5 – Garden Buildings

Once you have established a balanced layout for your garden, as we saw in the last chapter, the next step is to think about the buildings which go into it. These are generally the largest objects in the garden, and the most difficult to move, so it is worth getting them right before you move on to smaller objects and movable details such as planting.

You may already have garden buildings which you could move if necessary - or at least remedy any problems you have with them - or you might be intending to add new buildings to the garden. Possibly you may have one or two buildings already, such as a garden shed and a greenhouse, and be planning to add some other feature as well, such as a summerhouse or a pergola. In this chapter, I use the phrase 'garden buildings' to mean any large permanent or semi-permanent structure such as:

- tool sheds
- greenhouses
- gazebos
- summerhouses
- pergolas and walkways
- arches and bowers
- children's playhouses and tree houses.

Some of these buildings are functional, such as the tool shed, while some are purely decorative, such as a pergola. Some may even have a double role: a summerhouse can be an office during the day and a relaxing area for the family to use at weekends.

If you have a veranda or a conservatory, you may be wondering whether to feng shui it as part of the house or part of the garden. Again, this is a matter for your own intuition. How do you use it? And do you see it as part of the house or of the garden? These structures, which link the house and the garden, are generally good for feng shui. But you will have to decide for yourself whether yours belongs with the house or with the garden.

Positioning Garden Buildings

The first decision to make is where you want your building to be. It is no good putting a greenhouse in the most shaded part of the garden, and it is extremely frustrating to find that your tool shed is nowhere near where you will want to use the tools. So, for functional buildings especially, you have to be practical about locating them.

The most important considerations at this stage are not to create a cramped, overcrowded section of garden where the ch'i will be trapped, and not to create too much deep shade in an already shady part of the garden. Of course, any structure will create some shade, but try to make sure that you site the building where you can afford, or even want, more shade to create a better balance. Some buildings, such as gazebos and pergolas, exist in order to give shade, so you should put them in a part of the garden where shade would be welcome; this makes as much sense for you as it does for the ch'i.

The other question to consider at this stage is which enrichment the building will be best suited to. This will be affected by how you view the building and its function. Suppose you are siting a greenhouse. If you grow things to sell at the local market, you could put the greenhouse in your wealth enrichment. If you are growing young plants, the new beginnings area might be a good location. Or perhaps you particularly enjoy greenhouse gardening and see it as a luxury activity when you have the time - in which case the pleasure and indulgence enrichment would be a good location.

By the way, if you decide to site a building in a hidden-away corner where you cannot see it, perhaps because you think it is unattractive, the ch'i will not be able to reach it easily and will stagnate. This means that the building will be left virtually unused and you might as well not build it in the first place. By all means screen a building from the house if you prefer to, but make sure that it is freely accessible from other parts of the garden.

Size and Shape

The next consideration is the size and shape of the building, which of course interrelates with the question of position. A small building will not make an area seem as cramped as a large building might; a low structure will cast its shade over a shorter distance than a tall structure would. So when you decide where to put your building, you will already have given this some thought.

The general aim with all garden buildings is to opt for curved and rounded shapes rather than angular ones, unless the building is in an area which needs a straight-line remedy. Broadly speaking, make rose arches curved rather than straight across the top, and have a round or octagonal summerhouse.

Of course, a circular tool shed sounds a bit daft, but you can at least go for a square rather than rectangular design. And greenhouses often come in an octagonal shape nowadays. Other buildings, such as gazebos, lend themselves more readily to a round or octagonal shape.

Don't forget to consider the height of your structure as well as the length and breadth. A pergola often tends to be a long, narrow walkway. But all you have to do is increase the height and set the upright posts wider apart and you have a much better shape. Put arched rather than straight horizontal bars over the top, and you have an excellent feng shui design. People often put a pergola over a path which has a flower bed on one or both sides of it. But if you widen the pergola to cover the flower beds as well, you create a better proportion and you make the flower bed part of the feature.

If you do have an angular-shaped building - perhaps you have inherited a toolshed which you cannot realistically move - you can soften the shape by planting climbers, either on a trellis or straight up the building. Don't smother the building, though, or the ch'i will be unable to get inside it.

Make sure you keep the climber pruned so that you can still see the building and, especially, the entrance to it.

People often forget the shape of the roof, but it is an important part of the design. A tall, pointed roof can act as a straight-line remedy which directs the ch'i upwards, while a low, squat roof can prevent the ch'i circulating effectively inside the building. So keep the roof in proportion to the rest of the building.

In China, roofs are generally built with the eaves curved upwards. This slows the ch'i down so that instead of cascading off the edges, it flows gently down from the roof. This design is effective on summerhouses, pavilions and gazebos.

Materials

Try to match the materials you use to the part of the garden you are in, if possible. You can make garden structures from wood, from stone or from metal. Try to use wood in the east, stone in the centre (earth) area of the garden and metal in the west. In the fiery south, a building with plenty of glass to let the sun in is appropriate, and in the watery north you may not be able to create a building out of water, but you could perhaps incorporate a water feature into it (Chapter 6 is all about using water in the garden).

There are all sorts of other, less obvious materials you could use instead. How about decorating a building in the north of the garden with shells to symbolize the sea? Or putting plenty of candle sconces on the walls of your southerly summerhouse? If you cannot actually use the element for the part of the garden you are in, you can always represent it in this sort of way instead.

Remember to think about the materials you use on the roof of your building, too. You could use wooden slats or tiles, clay tiles, slate, an open roof with climbers trained over it, glass, metalwork ...
anything you choose. Find something appropriate to the part of the

garden you are in, and a material which is of a suitable colour, too.

Colour and Design

You can always paint your building, or stain it if it is made of wood,
or grow coloured foliage over it. Wooden buildings don't have to be
brown and even stone buildings, with the wide range of natural colours
available, can still be painted in another shade. If the feng shui around the
building is in balance, use a colour
(natural or applied) which suits the direction of that part of the garden:

- South and south-east
Bright red, orange, yellow and purple

- North
Blue and creamy white

- East and north-east
Green

- West and north-west
Soft yellow and bright white

- South-west
Rust, brown, deep red, plum, and dull yellow.

In places where the ch'i needs to be stimulated, bright colours, such as
yellow, orange, red, strong pink and purple, and sharp white, will help to
encourage it. If you want to soften and calm the ch'i, use soft blues and
pinks, creamy whites and other pastels.

When it comes to the general design of the building, you will have your
own opinion about what will suit its purpose. But it is important to ensure
that the ch'i can get inside the building easily so that it can flow around it
effectively. You will need to have plenty of windows, even in a tool shed,
to let the ch'i in and out. How many is plenty depends on the size of the

building; use your instinct to sense whether the ch'i can get in and out easily. Make sure any climbers or bushy plants are pruned regularly to prevent the windows or - especially - the door from becoming overgrown and inaccessible.

Open-sided buildings, such as many gazebos and summerhouses, or verandas, are exceedingly good for feng shui. The ch'i has easy access in and out of the building. Gazebos were originally developed in Persia, where they had a hole in the middle of the roof for viewing the stars at night. An open roof is, of course, another access route for ch'i, and therefore a particularly beneficial design.

TASK

Garden buildings are generally made from wood, stone, metal or glass. But your imagination may be 'able to come up with all sorts of alternatives. I have already mentioned decorating a

building with shells, but there are all sorts of other options such as thatching, for example.

Try to think of at least half a dozen other materials which you could use to make, or cover, a garden structure. Anything goes, apart from artificial materials such as concrete or plastic, which ch'i does not like.

CHAPTER 6 – Water in the Garden

The words feng shui mean 'wind' and 'water', and these are the two most basic elements of any garden with good feng shui. Any open-air garden will have wind moving through it, whether in gusts or gentle breezes. But you will need to make sure that your garden also incorporates water.

Ch'i loves water, and will be attracted towards it. Moving water will help to keep the ch'i active, while still water will calm it down. The only kind of water to avoid is stagnant, dirty water; so make sure any birdbaths or still ponds are cleaned out regularly.

There are several different sources you might get your water from, and you should aim to use natural water provided by nature. If you are lucky enough to have a natural stream or spring in your garden, use it. If not, try to use rainwater - perhaps collected in a water butt – rather than using tap water from the mains, as this is the least natural and beneficial source. However, a water feature which uses tap water is still far better than no water feature at all.

The Eight Remedies

Water is the principal feature of a garden which can be used, in one form or another, as any of the eight remedies. So you can always find a good spot for a water feature simply by identifying the places where you need a remedy - any remedy - and then choosing a watery solution to fit.

- Light

The surface of water is a natural reflector and can be used to bounce light into parts of the garden which need a light remedy. If the water is moving, it will create a more obvious rippling effect, so for a strong light remedy use a fountain or stream. You can increase the effect still further by hanging glass or silver balls, or crystals, around the water.

- Sound

A water feature which creates a noise will help to enliven stagnant ch'i in any part of the garden. Depending on the quality and depth of sound you want, you can create splashing, bubbling, gurgling, trickling or cascading noises using water.

- Colour

It is not a good idea to colour your water artificially with dyes, as this detracts from water's natural character, but you can create a colour remedy by using water to reflect - and therefore amplify - coloured foliage or flowers. Or line a pond or channel with coloured tiles, or place coloured glass pebbles or colourful stones at the bottom of a pond or a fountain. A fountainhead on the wall can incorporate painted wood or glazed tiles, or you could put a painted bridge over a stream. Even a simple ceramic birdbath can be glazed in an appropriate colour.

- Life Water attracts wildlife, from frogs and toads to dragonflies and water beetles. Birdbaths obviously encourage birds, or you could keep ducks on your pond. Goldfish are an obvious choice, too; the Chinese associate fish with money, so it is especially beneficial to keep goldfish in a pond in your wealth enrichment.

- Movement

Fountains, water jets, streams, water channels - all these features are excellent movement remedies. One of the best feng shui water arrangements is two or more pools connected by a stream, once again bringing movement to the area. But water - even still water - also attracts movement because it attracts wildlife.

- Stillness

To create a really good stillness remedy using water, you need not only still water but also a container for it which is a stillness remedy too. Use a stone-lined circular pool, or an old stone trough, or some similarly heavy and simple container to create the full effect.

- Functional device
 A fountain is a functional device, as is any water pump even if it is not visible (such as a pump for an artificial stream). Even a garden tap or a sprinkler, or a birdbath, will serve the purpose. You can always incorporate water into a functional device remedy if you want to.

- Straight line
A single water jet, either horizontally out from a wall or vertically up into the air, makes a straight line which can be used to remedy sluggish ch'i. You can also use a straight sided pond or a stone channel to keep water within straight lines if you need this sort of remedy.

Moving Water

If you have a water feature in which the water moves along a course, such as a stream or river, or a water channel you have constructed, you generally want it to meander gently in a curving path. If the water is moving too fast, or cascading too forcefully, it will stir up the ch'i and make it dangerous. If you have a natural stream or river running too fast through your garden, slow it down by opening part of it up into a larger pond, or breaking up one large cascade into several gentler ones.

A natural water course is unlikely to flow too straight, but if you have created your own water channel, make sure it meanders gently. The only exception to this is if you are trying to enliven the ch'i by speeding it up and bringing it into an area where it is otherwise prone to stagnate. But never do this in the west of the garden or you will provoke the White Tiger.

Water is an excellent way to calm the influence of the White Tiger in the west; a stream or pond in this part of the garden - or even a birdbath in a very small garden - will help to placate the Tiger and calm down the ch'i entering your garden from this direction.

If you have a water course which cuts your garden in two (or more), there is a danger that the areas of your life relating to the enrichments which are bisected will be separate. For example, if the stream or channel divides your relationship area from your children and family enrichment, your relationship is unlikely to produce offspring, or perhaps your family and your partner's will not integrate.

In order to prevent this happening, use plenty of bridges so that you never have to walk far to cross the water. Even if the channel is narrow enough to step over, you should still place symbolic bridges across it as well. Make sure, especially, that you use a bridge to link any enrichments which you particularly want to integrate.

Design and Materials

There is a wide choice of materials you can use to create a water feature, so find one which suits the relevant direction of the garden. Remember the elements which go with each part of the garden and incorporate them, if you can, into the feature:

- south: fire
- north: water
- east: wood
- west: metal
- centre: earth.

Use natural materials to complement the water in your garden. You can use coloured tiles, stones and cobbles, metal spouts and fountainheads, wooden or metal bridges over streams, earth banks and all sorts of other materials to create or add to your water feature. Banks can be made using sand or gravel and you can cover the floor of a pool with stones or cobbles. Avoid artificial materials, however, such as fibreglass, plastic and concrete, as ch'i dislikes these. If you must use such materials as pond liners, for example, make sure they are well hidden from all angles.

Consider putting an island in a large pool or a stream. This encourages the ch'i to flow in eddies and swirls, and adds interest to the garden. You could create a stone island, or an island planted with flowers, or you could simply find a beautiful old' boulder and position it in the middle of a stream so that the water has to flow around it.

When it comes to design, opt for curving shapes, of course. Formal ponds, birdbaths or fountain pools should be round or octagonal, or semi-circular if the pool is against a wall. A round pond in the centre of a garden is an excellent magnet to encourage the ch'i to flow right into the garden; make sure the size of the pond is in proportion to the rest of the garden.

And one more important point: remember to enjoy the water in the garden. Install a seat, or create a raised section of bank along the edge of a stream, so that you can sit beside the water and enjoy the sight and the sound of it, and the wildlife it attracts.

Safety

If you have small children you will, of course, want to be careful not to use any water features which might be unsafe for them. But this still leaves you with plenty of choice. For example, you could place rigid metal mesh half an inch below the surface of a pond so that children cannot fall in. Or you can use a fountain which bubbles up through stones or cobbles and seeps straight back down again so there is no standing water. You might have a water jet coming out from a wall which falls on to paving beneath and disappears down the cracks (into a tank from where it is pumped back up to the fountain head again). You could even have a water channel in which the water is only half an inch deep.

It is certainly important to consider child safety when you are installing a water feature of any kind, but you should find that there are still plenty of options. You could even have a simple birdbath raised high enough off the ground that a small child cannot reach it - but make sure the top section is firmly cemented to the plinth and be pulled down by a child reaching up to it.

Choosing the Right Water Feature for you

Consider whether the ch'i in your garden needs to be energized or calmed down. If it needs to be encouraged - perhaps if you have a shady garden to the north of the house - you will need a feature incorporating moving water. If it needs slowing down - perhaps the garden is in the west, or to the south of the house and at the bottom of a hill - you would be better off choosing a still water feature.

Of course, if you have a large garden, you can have more than one water feature; perhaps a fountain in the north and a still pool in the west. Water in the part of the garden south of the house is traditionally thought to be ideal, but if this is not possible, don't worry.

You may want to introduce water in a particular enrichment towards which you want to attract ch'i. If your life is too uneventful in a particular aspect - work is boring, or your relationships go nowhere, for example - put a moving water feature in the appropriate enrichment. If you want to relax or pacify one aspect of your life - perhaps your social life is too hectic and your pleasure and indulgence area needs calming down - use a still, cool water feature in this enrichment.

Once you have decided what kind of feature you need and where, think about the appropriate materials according to the direction of the garden you are in. Of course, you cannot build a feature out of fire, but you could put it somewhere which catches the light, or hang crystals around it, or create a grotto which you can light candles inside, out of the wind.

Beyond this, the choice of feature is really up to you. Just remember that the more vigorous the movement of water, the more it will accelerate the ch'i around it. But the final point is essential: make sure you end up with a water feature from which you derive pleasure yourself.

TASK

This is a mental process to go through before you choose a water feature for your garden. The point of it is to get your imagination firing by dreaming up water features you might not otherwise think of. Even though you are unlikely to use the features you come up with (although you might possibly), you will find it far easier to think of a suitable and original way of bringing water into your garden after going through this exercise.

Over the course of a few days, come up with a mental design for each of the following water features in your own garden:

- the largest water feature you can imagine which fits in your garden

- the most ornate or wacky water feature you can think of

- a water feature incorporating the fire element (excluding the suggestions, earlier in this chapter).

The only guidelines are that you must personally like the designs you are dreaming up and that, in your imagination, money is no object. Once you have completed this exercise, start to think realistically about a water feature for your garden while these daydream designs are still fresh in your mind.

CHAPTER 7 – Seats and Ornaments

So far we have looked at the basic shape and layout of your garden, and at the features which, once in place, are not easily movable - buildings and water features. The next elements to consider in your garden are those which you can move around if you want to or need to.

The first thing to consider is seating in the garden. It is important to sit and enjoy your garden from time to time, even if you also enjoy working in it. If you never relax in your garden, you are unlikely to relax in your day-to-day life; even if you like to be busy, relaxation time is necessary too. So make sure you can sit down comfortably in your garden and, if you are tempted to keep weeding and watering instead, make sure you have a seat which is so inviting that you cannot resist it.

Of course, you can have several seats in your garden, and if the garden is sizeable, you really should have several. Aim at least to be able to see all but the most secret corners of your garden from one seat or another. You may well want seats in different parts of the garden so you can catch the sun at different times of day.

Plan Your Seating

Think about where you want to sit. Do you want to be able to sit and keep an eye on the children when they are playing? Do you want to sit in private in a part of the garden which is not overlooked by neighbours? Do you want to be able to sit close to the kitchen door, so you can enjoy a few minutes outside here-and there even while you're cooking? There is no point putting a seat somewhere that you are not actually going to use it.

Next, consider what you want to do when you are sitting in your garden. If you want to take work out into the garden, you will probably need a table of some kind, whether it is an antique, wrought iron table or simply a suitable tree stump. If you want to meditate alone, a single seat will be ideal; whereas if you like sitting out with company, you will want several seats. And if you plan to eat out with friends, you will need to choose somewhere that can accommodate a good sized table, too, maybe close to the barbecue.

Do you like to sit in the sun? If so, there is no point in sitting your seat in a shady spot which never gets any direct sunlight. Equally, it would be silly to put a seat in full sunshine if you are more comfortable sitting in the shade.

Sitting in the Best Enrichment

The other point to consider is which enrichment you want your garden seat to be in. Just because you want to watch the kids playing, you don't necessarily have to put a seat in the children and family enrichment. You may be able to keep an eye on them perfectly well from a neighbouring enrichment, such as the relationship area. And once the children have gone to bed ... you have a romantic seat for you and your partner to sit out under the stars with a glass of wine.

If you want a seat where you can just sit and think, the wisdom and experience enrichment would be a good place to site it. If you want to meditate, perhaps you might choose your health and happiness area. If you do the kind of work which you can sometimes take out into the garden, the wealth area would be a good place for a seat. Maybe you want a group of seats for entertaining and sitting out with other people? How about the friends and new beginnings enrichment? Or even pleasure and indulgence?

If you enjoy doing all these things, you can have several garden seats. You can always double up some of them. If you have seats in your children and family enrichment for keeping an eye on the kids, you can also use them for sitting out with family or with your partner. A seat for working at could go into the wisdom and experience enrichment, and double as your thinking or meditation seat.

Designing Your Seat

It makes sense to match the seat to its purpose or location. If you want a romantic seat in your relationship enrichment, don't use a hard stone seat. Have a comfortable two-seater bench and construct a rose-covered arbour over it to give it beauty, scent, shade and privacy. If the seat is going into the children and family area you might want to paint it a cheerful colour, and choose something fairly low so small children can climb on to it easily. You could even find an old log and carve it into the shape of a crocodile or a dragon, with seating along its back.

Don't use synthetic materials for seating, such as plastic, as ch'i avoids them. Use natural materials, suited if possible to the part of the garden you are in - wood in the east, metal in the west and so on. As well as wood and metal you can make seats from stone or brick, you can form an earth bank to sit on, or you can create a herb seat by making a raised bed and then planting it with chamomile or thyme so that the scent is released when you sit on it. (Both these plants are tough enough to take being sat on; if you want a chamomile seat, use non-flowering chamomile and grow it in full sun.)

The shape of the seat you use will affect the flow of ch'i through and around it. Unless you want a straight-line remedy, use seats and benches which have a curving line to them. This doesn't mean the front edge cannot be straight, but try to use chairs with rounded backs, or benches with a curving, rounded metalwork design set into them. Slatted benches create a straight line which will accelerate ch'i, unless you cover the seat and back with cushions. Use straight designs only if you want to speed up sluggish ch'i.

An open design, such as fretwork or metalwork, gives the ch'i more opportunity to flow in, out of and around the seat, so it is a good thing. Natural objects used as seats - such as suitably shaped logs, tree stumps and even boulders (if you can find a comfortable one) are attractive to ch'i, and generally look very much in keeping with a good feng shui garden.

You can, of course, use colour to help your seating to fit into the direction of the garden in which it is sited. You can paint metal or wooden seats, and you can use natural materials in suitable colours. In the east, where green is the best colour, you could plant a turf seat or bank to sit on. If you plant a bower over your seat, use plants with suitably coloured flowers or foliage.

Suit Your Seats to its Surroundings

It is important to make sure that your seat blends into its surroundings. This does not mean that it should be invisible; simply that it should be in keeping. A brightly coloured seat in a children's area with lots of colourful toys will be ideal, while the same seat in a wild woodland garden would be jarring and would therefore provoke the ch'i to accelerate.

Always think about the area immediately around any seat or bench. The planting, or the ornaments around it, should give it a sense of belonging to the space it is in. This will influence the ch'i harmoniously. So a roughly hewn log would fit into a wild or woodland setting; a stone bench set on flagstones might look even more at home with a couple of stone or clay pots placed nearby; and a romantic seat under a rose bower might be painted in a pastel shade and be made of metal with a flower design wrought or embossed in it.

Choosing Ornaments and Statues

Although you can certainly use ornaments as remedies in your garden - and we will look at that in a moment - you are not obliged to. So long as they encourage gently flowing ch'i, you can have them anywhere you like. Natural materials are excellent, of course, such as wood, stone, crystal, iron and terracotta. As always, try to match the material to the direction of the part of the garden it is in. Go for rounded shapes such as pots, jars and urns, millstones, curving sculptures, round sundials and so on, and don't forget you can bring colour into the garden through any ornaments and sculptures you have.

Any reflective surface is good for feng shui, so long as you don't have too much light in the area already. This means mirrors, of course, which are also ideal for 'filling in' missing enrichments as we saw in Chapter 3. But you can also use other reflective surfaces – stainless steel planters, strings of crystals, or even glass or mirrored balls such as you might hang on a Christmas tree. If you are using this kind of ornament, however, make sure you keep it clean. It will be bad for the feng shui of the area if you allow it to become mud-spattered or covered in green algae.

If you are using sculpture, other than abstract sculpture, try to match the subject matter to the enrichment or direction you are putting it in. So a sculpture of children playing would be best sited in the children and family enrichment. A figure of Poseidon, Greek god of the sea, for example, could go in the north to symbolize water. A reproduction of Rodin's *The Thinker* would suit the wisdom and experience area.

Using Ornaments as Remedies

Statues and ornaments can be used to create just about any kind of remedy in the garden, and they will be there all year round, unlike many of the plants and flowers. Here is an idea of the kind of objects you could use to create remedies:

- Light
Mirrors or glazed tiles, glass balls, garden lights or lanterns all bring light into dark areas of the garden.

- Sound

Wind chimes create sound, of course, as do strings of pebbles hung up in groups, or strings of any other natural objects you can find.

- Colour
Glazed pots and statues, or painted wooden troughs and ornaments, all make excellent colour remedies.

- Life
You can use a birdbath or a bird table to bring life into the garden, or an ornamental urn containing a plant such as lavender which attracts bees.

- Stillness
Heavy old stone troughs, millstones and staddle stones all create stillness, as do large round objects such as earthen pots and stone balls. Statues can also make good stillness remedies; use one with a relevant theme - a statue of children in the children and family enrichment, or a stone owl in the wisdom and experience area.

- Movement
Wind chimes, again, or feathers threaded together, or a garden windmill, will all bring movement to the garden.

- Functional device
A sundial is an ornamental device, as is a garden windmill or a wind chime.

- Straight lines
Square or rectangular planters and troughs, and any statue which uses strong straight lines, help to revive stagnating ch'i.

TASK

In order to decide where to place seats in your garden, you need to go through a thought process to make sure the seat or seats end up where you are really going to use them. So work through the following exercise:

- Make a list of the places in the garden where you like to sit.

- Are there any seats in the garden you never use? Why not?

- Note down what you like to do while you are sitting in the garden (it may vary for each of these locations; if so, make a note of what you do where).

- What else do you need to perform these activities: sun, shade, a table or whatever?

- Do you like to sit in these places alone or in company?

- Are these seats in suitable enrichments for the activities you use them for?

- Are there other places in the garden where you would like to sit if you had a seat there? For example, would you like to have a seat in the relationship enrichment to encourage you and your partner to sit out together more often? Or is there a shady tree you would like to sit under if you had a seat?

By the time you have worked through this exercise, you should have a much clearer idea of which seats to keep, remove, or add to your garden.

CHAPTER 8 – Plants in the Garden

The mainstay of most gardens is the plants - trees, shrubs, climbers, flowers and vegetables. Apart from existing mature trees, however, they are also the most movable feature of the garden, which is why we have left them until last. Once the rest of the garden is designed, you can fill in all the gaps with plants. What's more, if you decide that you want to change it later, most plants are relatively easy to move around until you are happy with the arrangement.

Ch'i is attracted to life, so all plants are essentially good for the [eng shui of your garden. However, different plants affect ch'i in different ways, so you do have to make sure that you use each plant in an appropriate place. If it accelerates ch'i, use it in a sleepy, stagnant area, and use the most calming plants in places where the ch'i is inclined to be overactive.

Mature Trees

The older a tree is, the more strongly its own internal ch'i has developed. You should never remove old trees or other ancient plants - some climbers, for example, can reach great ages. If a mature tree happens to stand in your wisdom and experience enrichment, think yourself very lucky indeed.

You can prune old trees to keep them healthy, so long as you don't disturb them. Treat them with the greatest respect. If you really feel that your garden is totally overshadowed and you cannot live with the tree, I'm afraid the correct feng shui response is for you to move, rather than the tree.

Plant Shape

When choosing plants of any kind for your garden, the first thing to think about is their overall shape. As always, ch'i will be attracted to curving, rounded shapes, so aim to use as many plants as possible which have this shape. Oak trees are an excellent shape, as are apple trees; conifers tend not to be. When it comes to shrubs and tall plants, something like a magnolia is ideal, while a bamboo would be too tall and spiky. Some flowers, such as red-hot pokers, are much spikier than, for example, peonies. Use the spiky, straight plants and prickly or thorny plants in areas where the ch'i needs livening up, but avoid them elsewhere. (Roses are one exception to this, as we shall see in a moment.)

The next point to consider is the shape of the leaves and flowers. Holly trees are reasonably rounded in their overall shape, but their leaves are prickly and will accelerate ch'i. Don't use them in the west of your garden. Trees such as horse chestnut have rounded leaves, whereas willow leaves are pointed, despite the tree's overall shape.

You will probably be thinking that there are lots of plants with contradictory features: the overall shape is rounded, but the leaves are pointed, for example. When this is the case, assess the plant according to its most prominent aspect. Lavender, for example, does have spiky leaves, but the most obvious feature of the plant is its overall round, mound-like shape - especially if you clip it to encourage this - so the plant's net effect on the ch'i in your garden is to encourage it to flow harmoniously.

Roses are another example of a contradiction. The flowers and leaves are rounded, but the stems bear thorns. However, the negative effects of the thorns are outweighed by the positive benefits of the rest of the plant, so roses are on balance excellent for ch'i. Hollyhocks, delphiniums and foxgloves are all examples of flowers which have a tall flowering stem but rounded flowers. All of these are best avoided where the ch'i is overactive, but anywhere else the tall shape is well enough offset by the flowers so that you can grow these quite happily.

Plant **Colour**

Green plants are appropriate throughout the garden, although the east is a particularly good area for a collection of green plants – not only foliage but flowers, too. Try growing green hellebores, euphorbia, bells of Ireland, lady's mantle and green tobacco plants in the east to give you a variety of greens throughout the year. But green is a neutral enough colour to use anywhere.

In the rest of the garden, you can certainly mix colours, but allow the colour which suits the direction to dominate:

- South and south east Bright red, orange, yellow and purple
- North Blue and creamy white
- East and north-east Green
- West and north-west Soft yellow and bright white
- South-west Rust, brown, deep red and plum, dull yellow.

Remember that the garden will change throughout the year and that you will need to use a succession of flowers to keep the colour going for as much of the year as possible. And remember, too, that flowers are not the only way to bring colour to the garden through plants. Foliage, berries and even bark all contribute, and in the winter months these are often the best way to keep colour in your garden.

Scent

Beautiful scents always encourage ch'i and are excellent feng shui. Grow as many scented plants as you can and avoid unscented varieties of plants such as roses and lilies which are abundantly available in scented forms.

Scent is another factor which counts in favour of a plant and compensates for less beneficial factors such as spiky leaves. This is another reason why lavender is good for ch'i, and why even with its thorns, the rose is still an excellent plant to grow anywhere in your garden.

Plants in Winter

It is important to keep your garden alive throughout the winter, so grow winter-flowering plants such as yellow winter jasmine, red, white and pink japonicas, and witch hazel in wonderful tones of bronze, scarlet and yellow. Plant early bulbs such as snowdrops, *anemone blanda*, crocuses and early daffodils so that your garden has flowers throughout the year. Winter aconites can flower in January, as can hellebores, and primroses in a mild year. So there is no excuse for having a garden without life and colour in the winter, even if you have to look a little harder for it.

Many plants have wonderful coloured stems in winter, such as the bright scarlet stems of dogwood, yellow and green willow stems, and white and purple rubus. Plants with attractive bark such as eucalyptus or birch are shown off at their best in winter, too.

Evergreens are another mainstay of winter planting, but don't allow heavy, dark conifers to dominate your garden. Many of these - especially foreign varieties - are also a sterile environment which supports little or no wildlife. Use holly where the ch'i is sleepy, and yew if you want conifers. Don't forget all the evergreen shrubs which you can use, especially herbs such as rosemary and sage, which are excellent for feng shui.

Winter is a slower, sleepier time of year than summer, for us as well as for the garden. But we are not evolved to hibernate. We may slow the pace in winter, but we don't grind to a halt. Make sure the garden is awake all year, even if it less active in the winter months. Make sure there is always colour and shape, and a feeling that the garden is ready to spring into life as soon as the warm weather arrives.

Keep the garden tidy through the winter. Leave seed heads for the birds - you want to encourage them into the garden - but tidy up any dead leaves and stems, and clear away the empty flowerpots, children's toys, garden furniture and anything else which is cluttering the area or making it untidy.

It is no coincidence that most winter and early spring flowers are strongly coloured. The ch'i needs stimulating and these flowers have precisely this effect. So spread them around as much as you can, especially in the sleepier corners of the garden. You can also stimulate the ch'i with sharper, straighter shapes than you would at other times of year. For example, a dogwood, pruned to produce straight, brightly coloured stems in winter will stimulate ch'i. The same shrub later in the year will have oval leaves which soften the ch'i, and the stems will fade in colour and be less visible. So the same plant can produce very different effects at different times of year.

The ch'i from the west is still dangerous in winter, especially if your western boundary is more open in the winter. A deciduous hedge, for example, will let through more ch'i in the winter than in the summer. So avoid putting too many sharp or spiky plants, or too many straight-stemmed shrubs, in this part of the garden.

The ch'i from the Black Tortoise in the north, on the other hand, becomes so sleepy in winter it can stagnate altogether. So this is the part of the garden to plant your straight or spiky plants, and your brightly coloured daffodils and primulas.

Don't forget to think about the eight enrichments in winter, and try to keep each of them awake and active in some way. Here are a few suggestions:

- Fame
You will use this area every time you enter the garden. If your back garden is separate from the front and has its own fame area, make sure you visit the garden from time to time throughout the winter so that you use the fame enrichment.

- Health and happiness

Grow winter herbs, such as rosemary, in this part of the garden. It is also a good area for growing winter vegetables.

- Pleasure and indulgence

This is the place to grow something really beautiful and plentiful, with no purpose but enjoyment. Plant masses of spring bulbs here, to create a fertile riot of life in early spring. Or grow a particularly wonderful, favourite plant, which is at its best in the colder part of the year. Make it something heavily scented, such as a winter-flowering honeysuckle.

- Friends and new beginnings

Plant plenty of spring bulbs here to herald the new beginning of the warmer weather.

- Relationship

If you and your partner both enjoy being in the garden in winter, spend time in this area. If not, grow plants here which will blossom and bear fruit even in the winter months.

- Children and family

Children like to play outside all year round, so encourage them into this area with a cosy playhouse or activities which will keep them warm - a swing and a slide, or space to play with a ball. Whether or not you have children, you can extend your circle to include a whole family of birds if you put out nuts, seeds, bread and scraps for them in the cold weather. This is a good enrichment for a bird table.

- Wisdom and experience

A compost heap in this area will mature throughout the winter, even if you cannot see it happening, and you can visit it from time to time with kitchen waste to add to it.

- Wealth

Store any garden furniture or equipment here, so the enrichment has a use throughout the winter.

TASK

Most of us, when we choose the plants to put in our garden, select them on the basis of how much we like them before we start to think about feng shui, soil suitability, frost resistance and all the rest. If you want a good feng shui garden, you can still do this.

- Make a list of your favourite plants that you really want to have in your garden.

- Note down which parts of the garden each could grow in- sun or shade, damp or dry and 'so on

- Now go through your list and write beside each plant which enrichments it could physically grow within in your garden - which have the right growing conditions.

- Next, by each plant, note down its shape and its colouring (including foliage or berries if these are significant).

- Now write down which direction these plants are best suited to - avoid spiky plants in the west, use bright red and orange flowers in the south, and so on.

- Match up your list of enrichments and of directions, and you will find out where in the garden you can grow the plants you like best. Some will have several options, while others may be limited.

Use this information as a reference when planning your planting scheme. You don't have to stick to the letter of it; just keep the bulk of the plants in the right areas of the garden. For example, if your health and Happiness enrichment is in the west, and this is where you want a herb garden, it would be ridiculous to suggest that you cannot grow chives because they are spiky. Just grow them next to a more rounded plant such as sage, and keep lavender, rosemary and other spiky-leaved plants pruned into rounded shapes.

CHAPTER 9 – Difficult Gardens

Most of us are not lucky enough to have square or circular gardens. In fact, many of us have gardens which are positively difficult shapes in terms of encouraging ch'i to flow around them. In Chapter 2, we looked at how to remedy some of the problems associated with this kind of garden, and how to overlay the Pah Kwa on to the plan. We also saw what the implications were for your life, and how the irregular shape of your garden influences the area of your life to which each enrichment applies.

But there are general rules which apply to designing the layout of difficult gardens, regardless of which way the Pah Kwa falls. Ch'i likes to flow in curves and to be free and expansive whichever enrichment it is in. So there are certain general guidelines to follow when you have a difficult garden, whatever the precise problem with it. You should think about these overall principles when you first design - or redesign - your garden, before you go on to think about the specifics of how you will use each enrichment. You can then adapt the basic approach to suit those specific requirements.

The Guidelines

- The aim in all gardens with difficult shapes is to reduce the impact of the shape which the ch'i doesn't care for, and replace it with the appearance of a more ch'i-friendly shape. So you need to make a long, thin garden seem shorter and wider, for example. This will encourage the ch'i to enter and flow around it.

- As always, you are aiming for curves and spaces and trying to avoid impenetrable corners. Smooth off sharp edges and corners with plants and climbers, or with garden ornaments.

- Once you have worked out the best layout for your garden, you can start to fill in the details with features which suit the enrichments. You can put benches, a herb garden, the children's swing or the barbecue in the most appropriate places.

Other Difficulties

Sometimes the problem with a garden doesn't lie in its shape, but in some other feature of it. Perhaps it is heavily shaded, or very small. In this case, the aim is still to create the opposite impression in order to encourage the ch'i. You can add light to a shady garden, shade to a garden which is too bright and exposed, and make a small garden look bigger.

All these difficulties can be resolved if you apply a little thought and imagination to how you can counteract the negative influences of your garden.

The Examples

The examples which follow are just that: examples. They are not prescriptions for exactly what you must do if your garden has this or that problem. They are simply ideas to illustrate how such difficulties can be overcome, and to help you come up with ways to improve the feng shui of your own garden.

Since the ideas which follow are general ones, the example gardens have not been attributed directions or enrichments. The overall shape or style is the important thing, but you can move features around to suit your own circumstances. A bench could be made to suit the element which governs the part of the garden it is placed in - wood in the east, for example. Or, in your own garden, you might replace the bench with a potting shed or a child's sandpit to suit the enrichment.

So take the ideas you find on the following pages as inspiration for coping with an ostensibly problem garden, and adapt them as you wish.

Long, Thin Gardens

The long, thin garden is a common feature of town and city gardens in particular. Not only is the garden badly proportioned, it is usually very squared off in design, with narrow, straight flowerbeds down each side a typical layout. These flower beds are often backed by uncompromisingly bare fences or walls. This accentuates the shape and creates an overexposed and boring garden which is, therefore, unwelcoming to ch'i as well as to us.

The key to dealing with a long thin garden is to:

- divide it into separate areas
- introduce curves
- add height.

This will add interest to the garden and encourage the eye, and the ch'i, to explore it. Make sure each area you create is easily accessible from any other - don't connect them with narrow, dark entrances - but ensure that the whole garden isn't visible from the back door. If it is, what is the point of exploring it? You can see it all without moving.

In the example opposite, you can see that these features have been used to create the appearance of a wider and more interesting garden:

- the patio and circular lawns create an appearance of width
- the garden has been divided into clear areas

- the height either side of the rose arch creates a partial screen which draws the eye through the arch, and ensures the whole garden cannot be seen from the back door
- the arch is wide enough to avoid creating a narrow funnel for ch'i; there is an open and free-flowing feel to the whole garden
- the circular bed beyond the arch creates a private area where a bench can be placed to enjoy the peace and privacy.

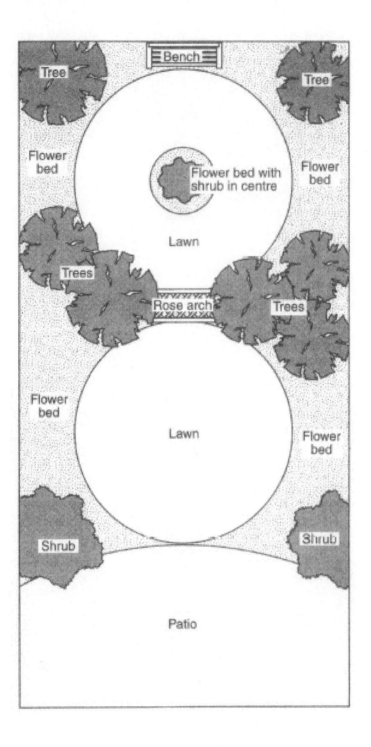

L-Shaped Gardens

Some L-shaped gardens aren't a problem. If the whole garden is visible from the entrance they are generally quite easy to deal with. But some L-shaped gardens have a section which is tucked away around a corner, and this type is all too often treated as two different gardens. The part which can't be seen from the garden entrance is frequently neglected, and the sharp corners which cut it off from the rest of the garden also discourage ch'i or even antagonize it.

If you have an L-shaped garden such as this, you need to

- bring the 'L' section into the rest of the garden
- smooth off any sharp corners
- use a device such as a mirror to recreate the 'missing' part of the garden.

This will create a unified garden which invites you into the '1' section rather than cutting it off. You can also give the 'L' section a special function to encourage its use; depending on the enrichment put your vegetable garden here, or the children's play area (if they're big enough you don't need to keep an eye on them from the kitchen window), or an area for sitting in the evening sunshine.

The example here has used several techniques to create the desired effect:

- the shape of the path treats the whole garden as a single space
- the lawn echoes this by continuing into the 'L' rather than giving way to some other surface as it turns the corner
- the sharp corners have been smoothed to encourage the ch'i to follow the gentle curve of the garden
- an arched trellis against the wall surrounds a trompe l'oeuil mural which creates the illusion of the 'missing' part of the garden.

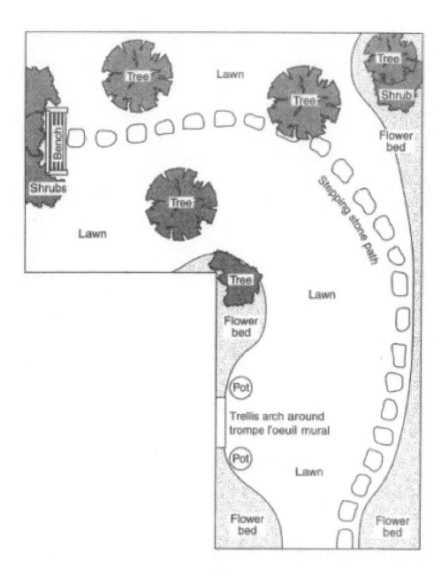

Heavily Shaded Gardens

The obvious solution to heavy shade, as we've seen earlier, is to reduce it by cutting back and pruning the overhanging branches, and perhaps even removing trees - although mature trees should be left as they have their own vital feng shui developed over decades or even centuries. But sometimes the trees aren't yours to prune and perhaps some of them are too mature and established to remove without damaging the feng shui.

The solution to this problem is to:

- bring more reflected light into the garden in the form of mirrors, glass baubles, metal sculptures and so on
- use outdoor electric lights and/or candles
- use light coloured materials for paths and paved areas, such as gravel or light brick
- raise some of the levels in the garden to bring you closer to the daylight

The example opposite turns a darkly shaded area into an interesting garden with many lighter areas. Although this kind of garden will never be bathed in sunlight, it can be dotted and dappled with areas of light which draw the ch'i around it:

- the main path draws the ch'i around the garden and is made of pale-coloured brick to bring a lighter tone to the garden
- the garden contains plenty of raised decking areas, with a linking walkway - if you can't bring the light to yourself, you can bring yourself closer to the light
- outdoor electric up lights around the garden can be turned on earlier in the evening than in a more open garden, and will bring a magical quality to the garden at night
- a pond brings reflected light to the garden, including a sculpture made from mosaic mirror tiles
- a metal slide in the children's corner reflects light.

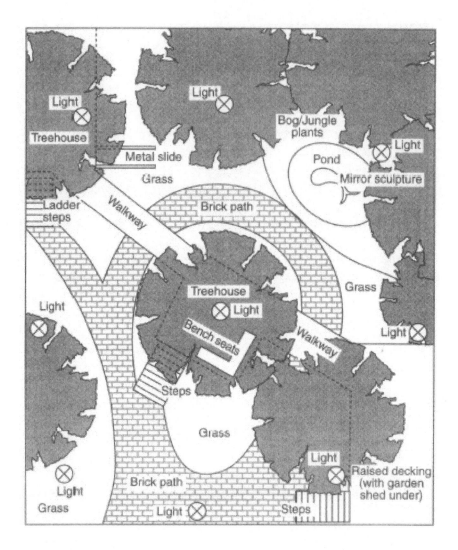

Light
Treehouse
Light
Metal slide
Grass
Ladder steps
Walkway
Light
Brick path
Light
Grass
Steps
Grass
Light
Grass
Brick path
Light

Bog/Jungle plants
Pond
Light
Mirror sculpture
Grass
Treehouse
Light
Bench seats
Walkway
Light
Light
Raised decking (with garden shed under)
Steps

Backyards

Backyard type gardens are small and often surrounded by high walls. They are frequently the only garden for the house, too, which means they have to house dustbins and they often collect all sorts of other junk too. These kinds of garden all too often look a mess; but they don't have to.

The techniques for bringing good feng shui to a backyard are:

- keep it simple and uncluttered
- paint the walls or fences if you need to bring in more light
- have a water feature, however small
- if you can't avoid dustbins or other clutter, screen them
- give yourself somewhere to sit and enjoy the garden
- enclosed gardens are great for trapping smells - make the most of this by using scented plants

In the example opposite a simple backyard has been turned into a peaceful area to enjoy:

- the overall design is simple and the open space in the middle of the backyard gives an uncluttered feel
- the walls have been painted a soft, pale colour to add light and a feeling of space
- the dustbins have been screened by a trellis with a scented climber growing up it
- grass is hard to maintain in a small space, so it has been replaced with brick paving
- a small fountainhead on the wall spills into a pond bringing sound and water into the small space
- herbs for cooking and for their scent are planted in simple pots
- the flower bed is small but gives ample opportunity to bring colour, life and scent to the garden
- a bench outside the backdoor means that the owner can sit and enjoy the sights, sound and scents of the backyard.

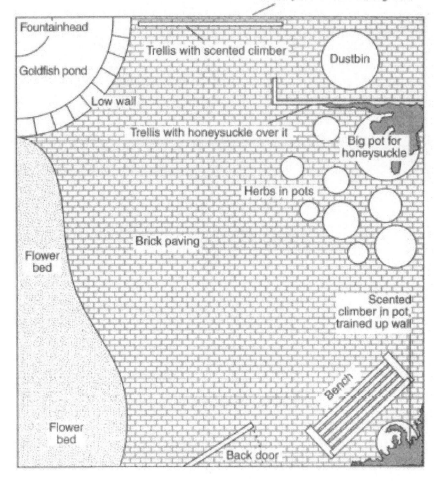

Walls painted soft blue/green

Fountainhead

Goldfish pond

Trellis with scented climber

Dustbin

Low wall

Trellis with honeysuckle over it

Big pot for honeysuckle

Herbs in pots

Flower bed

Brick paving

Scented climber in pot, trained up wall

Bench

Flower bed

Back door

CHAPTER 10 - Gardens with a Purpose

Many gardens have several functions to perform. They serve as a place for the kids to play but, once the kids have gone to bed, they get used by the parents to entertain their friends. Perhaps one corner of the garden is given over to growing vegetables, and another part provides a sitting area for relaxing in.

But sometimes a garden really has only one primary purpose and, when this is the case, it gives you the opportunity to design the layout of the entire garden with this in mind. You can give the whole plot over to the kids or, if you don't have children, perhaps you want to create a space which is yours alone to retreat to when you want to relax. Maybe your garden is a place for entertaining people, or maybe it is somewhere romantic to sit outside with just one special person.

In many ways it is a luxury to be able to design this kind of garden, as anyone whose garden has to fulfil a dozen functions will tell you. But it is also a great feng shui opportunity, since it makes it far easier to create a consistent, coherent style throughout the garden, which is far more inviting to ch'i than a bitty garden which can appear broken into several distinct sections if you're not careful.

Gardens with a single purpose are often smaller gardens; it's a style which lends itself to city and town gardens rather than to rambling country acres, where you have the space to give over different parts of the garden to different functions. But some larger plots can contain a garden within a garden; where this is the case the guidelines in this chapter can easily be adapted.

Guidelines

- If you are designing your garden for a single purpose, the first thing you will need to do is to consider where each enrichment falls. You need to make the best use of the space by placing each of the features you use in the most beneficial place.
- Don't forget the natural conditions either. If you mostly sit out in the garden in the evening, put the sitting area somewhere it will catch the evening sun. If this isn't the obvious place in terms of the enrichment it falls in, use the next enrichment round, or use remedies as we have seen earlier in the book to make the area more harmonious.
- Before you start to plan the layout of the garden, list the features you want to include in it. Remember, with only one purpose for the garden you can find more room for such features than you could if the garden had other functions as well.
- Now work out the most suitable enrichment for each of these features to fall in. You may have to juggle a few around as you go along, but this is the starting point for planning the layout.

The Example

As in Chapter 9, the examples which follow are simply suggestions to give you ideas. Your garden may have a different purpose, or the enrichments may fall in a different place. But each example begins with a list of features such as you might draw up yourself, and then shows how they are allocated to the most appropriate enrichment.

Regardless of how similar they are to your own garden, these examples should inspire you to find your own way to create a garden with a purpose which maximizes the beneficial forces of feng shui and creates a harmonious space for you to enjoy.

A Garden for Entertaining

Whether you enjoy weekend family lunches out of doors, a barbecue with the neighbours or an elegant al fresco dinner, your garden can be designed to maximize its potential as an outdoor room for entertaining. For this example, here is a list of features you might want in such a garden:

- an eating area
- a food preparation and serving area
- separate seating around the garden
- a barbecue
- lighting for evening entertaining
- attractive plants and flowers to enjoy
- a water feature with the sound of gentle running water to relax and entertain guests.

As you can see, the example opposite incorporates all these features. It has plenty of space, and two separate benches as well as the seating around the table. There is also a children's corner for entertaining children or families with young children. Both the eating area and the pond have electric lighting so the garden can be used in the evening, and plenty of space has been given over to preparing and eating food.

Some of the features have been carefully allocated to the most suitable enrichments:

- Herbs are in the health and happiness area. This also makes them handy to pick fresh for adding to salads and barbecues in the neighbouring food preparation area.

- The food is cooked and served in the pleasure and indulgence enrichment; just the place to ensure appetizing and enjoyable food.

- The table itself is in an open-sided but covered area so that a little rain doesn't spoil the fun. This is in the friends and new beginnings area, so it's an ideal place to sit down and entertain.

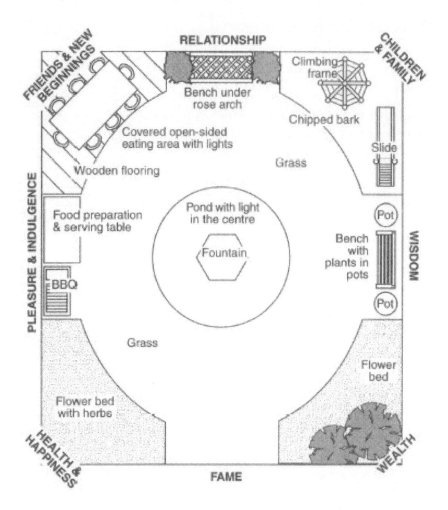

A Garden for Children

Many people's gardens are completely taken over by the children whether they like it or not. If this applies to you, why not make the most of it? Create a child's paradise, and then you'll at least get pleasure from watching them enjoy it. You can give children far more than simply a sandpit and a swing. The kind of features you might want in this garden includes:

- an area for children to grow their own plants
- an area to attract birds to the garden
- a swing and slide
- a sandpit
- a playhouse
- a treehouse
- an open space for playing games
- children's seating.

The centre of this garden is left open to give the children plenty of space to play. The pleasure and indulgence area is home to the football goal, but cricket stumps or a basketball net would do just as well. The pool and sandpit are near the house, so smaller children can be watched more easily, and the water in the pool is kept to only an inch in depth - just right for paddling without being a safety hazard. The garden features have been placed in harmonious enrichments:

- In friends and new beginnings, spreading into the relationship area, the area for children to grow their own plants has been combined with the playhouse to create a house and garden for them, complete with a seating area on their own scale.

- Children often see tree houses as a secret place, where they are a remove away from the grown-ups and they can learn to be more independent. The tree house therefore suits the wisdom area very well.

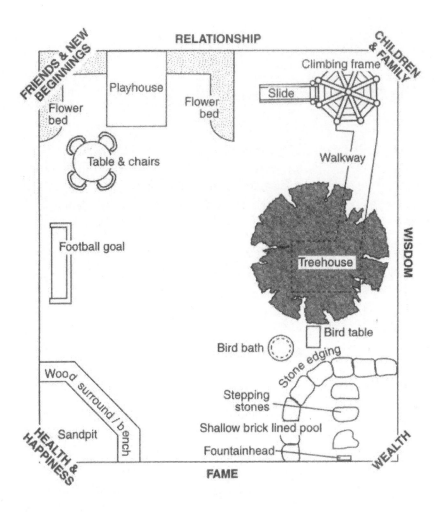

A Romantic Garden

If you like to entertain just one or two people at a time, especially your partner, you may want to give your garden over completely to romance. An old-fashioned, romantic garden creates a peaceful and happy atmosphere - which is ideal for encouraging ch'i as well as for enticing your lover. This kind of garden will also be delightful to spend time in alone.

Here are some features you might choose for a romantic garden:

- a bower seat
- an intimate dining area
- a still pool
- a wooden swing in a tree
- old-fashioned plants
- plenty of scented flowers
- a sense of mystery, such as half-hidden areas of the garden.

This example shows a garden which has a number of separate 'rooms'. Only the bower area at the far end is completely screened from the house, giving real privacy to the romantic seat with beds of scented flowers on either side. The dining area is partly screened by the lavender hedge, and with the pergola over it as well it has an intimate feel. The rose garden is also a separate 'room', echoed by the more open herb garden opposite.

- Eating in the pleasure and indulgence area is ideal, with the senses further stimulated by the scent of jasmine, honeysuckle and roses climbing over the pergola, and the view down the path of the pool at the centre of the garden.

- The bower seat is in the relationship enrichment, making it the perfect place for a private tryst.

- The swing in the tree, in the wisdom area, is an ideal place to sit and dream.

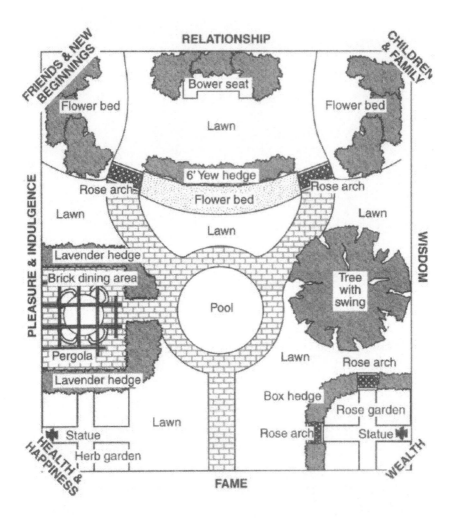

Printed in Great Britain
by Amazon